FIRE LOOKOUTS

VOLUME TWELVE

Vandals, Thieves & Firebugs

La Vaughn Vanderburg Kemnow

Mountains West Publishing

~

ISBN: 978-0-9996067-5-9

All historical information in this book is from original sources, the result of

years of dedicated research by Ron Kemnow for his web page

ronkemnow.weebly.com

Member, Forest Fire Lookout Association

Historical data presented in its original form, without comments

This series is not intended to be a complete history of fire lookouts, but rather to provide a glimpse, or overview, of what it was like to build, staff, and maintain the lookout system

"I have cheerfully retained the spelling, punctuation and capitalization of the original sources."

September 5, 1911: "Another fire was reported by the look-out on Custer Peak [Black Hills National Forest, South Dakota] about 10 o'clock Saturday night, who located it at the site of some cabins owned by Albert Steel of Lead, on Elk Creek. Ranger Smith was notified and was on the scent with a force of men and had the fire under control by 1 o'clock Sunday morning. The fire destroyed the Steel cabin is supposed to have been of incendiary origin." *(Deadwood Pioneer-Times)*

August 31, 1912: A fire report which reads like a detective story has just been received at the San Francisco office of the Forest Service.

At five o'clock on the morning of July 26, the lookout stationed on Bald Mountain, on the Sierra National Forest, sighted a fire on the south slope of Kaiser Crest. The District Ranger was immediately notified by telephone, and with a fireguard started for the fire at once. With much difficulty, it was put out. Investigation showed that it had started from a camp fire. On a quaking asp nearby were carved the names of W.B. and N.P. Gillespie and J.S. Pisor, all of Fowler, with the date July 25. The Forest Ranger immediately took their tracks and followed them into the valley. They were located in Fresno where on July 29 in Judge Graham's court they pleaded guilty to a violation of State Fire Law and were each fined $25, which upon their pleading poverty was reduced to a total of $30. *(Mountain Democrat* – Placerville*)*

Bald Mountain

Sierra National Forest, California

July 16, 2011 – Ron Kemnow Photo

April 26, 1916: "Nelson Woodward began his duties the first of the week as watchman on the forest fire lookout tower on Mount Massaemet [Franklin County, Massachusetts]. The state desires to take over the tower so as to control and protect it from the vandalism of mischievous boys, who have done considerable damage each year since the glass top was put on. The tower is the property of the citizens of the village, and is controlled by a committee, with whom the state has been unable to make satisfactory arrangements as yet." *(Greenfield Recorder)*

January 1917: "While at Bald Knob lookout [Siskiyou National Forest, Oregon] it was ascertained that someone had forced the lock helped himself to food and bedding inside, and carried away or misplaced the axe. This has happened each winter. It is hoped that a suitable lookout building on the lookout point, government property may be stored there, leaving the cabin open for transient hunters during the winter." *(The Siskiyou Bulletin)*

August 18, 1917: "A unique plan for the protection of the grain crop in the Klickitat valley against incendiary fires has been arranged by the Klickitat Council of Defense. A telephone line will be run to the top of the highest of the Twin Buttes [Washington] two miles east of Goldendale, commanding a view of the entire Klickitat valley wheat belt, and a guard will be stationed on the summit of the butte every night for the next thirty days, to keep a lookout for fire." *(The Colville Examiner)*

1918 and 1919: A tower, "consisting of an iron framework about 25 feet high surmounted by a small wooden house, reached by an iron ladder" was built on Catoctin Mountain in Maryland. The lookout was finished in November 1918; early in December the house was burned and the iron structure was damaged 'by an unknown incendiary.' Frequent incendiary fires were reported in the area, 'attributable in part to the firing of the woods to improve growth of huckleberries, and in part to general cussedness'

A new plan was underway to build a new steel tower several miles north, near a residence, to be completed for the spring fire season of 1920." *(State Board of Forestry Report for 1918 and 1919)*

September 21, 1920: "Much damage is being done to the beauty spots on Larch mountain [Mt. Hood National Forest, Oregon] and on the trail leading to that scenic point establishment of a permanent lookout there has been suggested as a remedy. The Trails club cabin on the summit has been partially destroyed. The pinnacle has been whitewashed, campfires have been left burning, initials have been carved on trees and painted on rocks and the entire trail has been left littered with picnic materials." *(Oregonian)*

November 28, 1920: "Hopes for the cessation of diminution of Larch mountain [Mt. Hood National Forest, Oregon] depredations is reflected in the combined efforts of the Mazamas, the Trails club, the forest service, the Crown-Willamette Paper company and other organizations and individual interests in the preservation of the famous mountain.

Last Sunday several members of the Mazamas, headed by Vincent Stroop, obliterated the white paint that has marred the beauty of the pinacle for two months or more, by covering it with a soft gray paint, closely akin to the color of the rock.

The Trails club cabin built for the shelter of mountain climbers is beyond repair, with half its sides and roof torn off for firewood.

The trees cut from the summit by vandals cannot be replaced.

Vandals have already this fall broken into the government cabin and the Crown-Willamette cabin below the summit.

Last spring, through congressional legislation as a result of agitation initiated by the Trails club, Larch mountain was included within the boundaries of the Oregon national forest. Larch mountain will not, however, be a part of the national forest until the government has exchanged land elsewhere for the private holdings. At present the government owns nothing but the trail right of way and a small area on the summit immediately surrounding the government cabin.

Efforts are being made to curb vandalistic inroads upon the mountain this winter by the paper company and the forest service, which are cooperating in paying a man to patrol the top and which have called upon other parties to help meet the expense." *(The Oregon Daily Journal)*

October 28, 1921: "Five fires in one batch were reported near the fire tower on Blue Knob, Bedford county [Pennsylvania], and there were evidences that all had been caused by incendiaries. Fire fighters succeeded in subduing the flames before much damage resulted." *(The Kane Republican)*

November 11, 1921: "The repair of the cabin on Larch mountain [Mt. Hood National Forest, Oregon] is being rapidly accomplished through the council of Oregon Outing clubs. Financing of the project is being handled chiefly by the Trails club, which built the cabin in the first place, and the Mazamas. The greater part of the work is being done by Barney Edwards, employed by the forest service and the Crown-Willamette Paper company, to stay on the mountain this winter to prevent vandalism.

A small party of men last Sunday, headed by Ray Conway and H.W. Erren of Larch mountain committee, assisted Edwards by packing up shakes from the Palmer road, a mile and a half to the summit.

The Larch mountain cabin, built and dedicated by the Trails club to the use of the climbing public, was almost demolished during the last few years by vandals who broke out the windows and tore off portions of the roof and walls for firewood. The council of Outing clubs is repairing the roof and putting in new windows so that the building will again be a shelter from storms for those who climb the mountain in winter. Edwards will act as caretaker, and will furnish wood to the public at a small charge." *(The Oregon Daily Journal)*

June 7, 1922: "Benson Polytechnic school hikers have protested to Supervisor T.H. Sherrard of the Oregon national forest at the aspersion placed on them because of vandalism said to have been committed a few weeks ago on the Crown-Willamette company's cabin on Larch mountain

[Mt. Hood National Forest, Oregon], which resulted in Sherrard's threatening to close the Larch mountain trail to the public.

The Benson boys pleaded not guilty to the charge, and stated that it was a Benson teacher who was with other boys not students at Benson, who did the damage. They also stated that the damage has now been fully paid.

The information previously given Sherrard from the representative of the Crown-Willamette company was that a group of Benson students, together with a Benson teacher, broke into the cabin by chopping a hole in the roof and did other damage amounting in all to about $60, which they then refused to pay." *(The Oregon Daily Journal)*

June 26, 1922: "A lighted cigarette stub cast aside by a careless camper in the vicinity of Pringle butte started a forest fire which was first glimpsed by the lookout at Paulina Peak [Deschutes National Forest, Oregon], when it had spread over an area of nearly a quarter of an acre. Forest employes yesterday afternoon had the blaze under control." *(The Bend Bulletin)*

June 1922: "In repairing the Bear Camp [Siskiyou National Forest, Oregon] telephone line we had to leave long stretches of wire buried under the snow and build a new line over the top. We found the cabin broken into as per usual and most of the equipment either moved out or knocked down so that the rats could destroy it. The lookout house was shaken a bit, most of the ceiling off, a window broken and the new fire finder rusted beyond all recognition. Outside of that everything was okey." *(The Siskiyou Bulletin)*

September 11, 1922: A portion of a letter published by the Cape Cod Chamber of Commerce [Massachusetts] to the Adjt. General complaining about damage to private and State property caused by the troops in their training exercises:

"3. At some time during the encampment, exact date unknown, a battery and mounted men drove through the State Forest Reservation on Shoot-Flying Hill and destroyed a very large number, estimated at 1000, of five-year old Scotch pine, set out by the Commonwealth. The troops were warned that it was a State Reservation by the Forest Fire Observer on the spot." *(Boston Daily Globe)*

Shoot Flying Hill

Barnstable County

Massachusetts

Postcard, Postmarked 1920

Ron Kemnow Collection

October 25, 1923: "Property stolen from the Aristes, Columbia County [Pennsylvania], fire tower, which was dynamited recently, has been recovered at the home of 'Teddy' Jackson and John Larkins at Centralia. Offers of settlement had been made, but the State is disposed to prosecute because this is the second instance where these public safeguards have been ruined by vandals." *(The Wilkes-Barre Record)*

June 25, 1924: "One forest fire was reported during the last 24 hours at the office here of Klamath Forest Protective Association [Oregon]. The blaze spotted late yesterday afternoon from the lookout on Chase Mountain was in the upper reaches of the Spencer Creek district above Upper Bridge. A ranger from the local office went out and the blaze was extinguished. It is believed to have been started by a camper. The relative humidity was at 33 this afternoon which is near extreme danger conditions." *(The Evening Herald)*

Chase Mountain

Klamath County, Oregon

c. 1936

Ellnora Young Collection

Pictured is Sam Rose

July 22, 1924: "$25.00 Reward for information leading to arrest and conviction of the parties who broke into the Brush Mountain [Blair County Pennsylvania] Fire Tower Cabin." *(Altoona Mirror)*

August 4, 1924: "Some years ago the State Forestry Department [Pennsylvania] - now the Department of Forests and Waters - erected a fine fire tower on the top of Blue Knob, in Bedford county just across the line of Blair county. The tower was erected so that employes of the department could scan a great scope of country, detect forest fires when they started and get out the fire fighters to extinguish these fires. The addition of the tower gave a greater protection to the woodland areas within its view, land owned by the state and individuals as well. Every citizen was a partner in the tower for the interests of every taxpayer were conserved through the agency of the tower by reason of the fact that forest lands were guarded. Every citizen was a joint owner in that tower; all citizens benefited alike in forest conservation.

But - a recent investigation has shown that the doors on both the cabin and the tower of the Blue Ridge forest fire observation tower in the Buchanan Forest District were torn from the hinges. The shutters over the cabin windows were damaged and most of the window panes were broken. The telephone was torn and considerable other damage was done about the tower.

It is hoped that the culprit or culprits can be found. Special efforts ought to be made to acquaint those responsible for these despicable acts with prison bars." *(Altoona Tribune)*

October 1924: "A miserable miscreant with a mania for collecting souvenirs has knocked off the brass cap, marking the elevation and name of Tiffany Peak [National Forest, Washington], and made away with it." *(Six Twenty-Six)*

April 15, 1925: "Boys, members of hiking parties traveling over the mountain sections in the vicinity of Altoona, are causing a great damage to the young timber according to reports made today by forest wardens and fire wardens who have visited in practically every section of the county during the past few weeks.

The wardens report that boys are using hatchets to chop down small trees for no apparent reason other than to exercise in chopping the trees. One of the wardens, on a walk from the fire tower on Brush mountain [Blair County, Pennsylvania] to the Kettle road yesterday, found a large number of trees cut right along the trail.

Announcement is made today by the wardens that all boys caught in the woods carrying hatchets will be relieved of the instruments. The wardens explain that there is no necessity for anyone to carry a hatchet on a hike, Boys Scouts can use the hatchets when a scoutmaster is along to supervise its use." *(Altoona Mirror)*

August 5, 1926: "After darkness had settled over the forest, at 9 o'clock the Black Butte lookout [Deschutes National Forest, Oregon] notified the central platting agent in Bend that flames were visible in the timber near the Allingham Ranger Station. From Bend went instruction to the Allingham station to send a fire guard to investigate the reported fire.

When the guard arrived at the place where the fire was located, it was found that campers had built a huge bonfire and were having a general good time in its light and warmth. They had failed to notice that their permit specified that a fire only large enough for cooking and for providing a reasonable amount of heat should be built.

No arrests were made, but campers learned that a bonfire can disturb the rest of a far reaching fire control organization." *(The Bend Bulletin)*

March 30, 1927: "The state department of forests and waters in 1923 erected a 60 foot steel fire tower on Brush mountain [Blair County, Pennsylvania] northeast of this city (Altoona). Near its base was erected a steel cabin for the forest ranger. A ranger is kept on the job there during the fire period which usually is April and May, October and November.

This ranger keeps a close watch on the surrounding country, is in touch with fire wardens by telephone and in a general way safeguards the property of the public. He also has on hand, at all times, literature concerning conservation and educational matters pertaining to reforestation and forest fire fighting.

It is a matter of sincere regret, then, to think that any person would be low and mean enough to go there, in the absence of the ranger, and destroy what the state has built up. On a number of occasions, men or boys or both, have visited the place and did inestimable damage to the tower, the cabin and the trees.

The fire tower and the cabin are anything but targets for rifle practice, yet some people think it a great 'joke' to put a bullet through. Not only have both the cabin and the tower and the observation station on the tower been 'shot up' but they have been rifled and otherwise destroyed.

Several arrests have been made. The last ones arrested, three boys, were hailed before a magistrate and a fine and costs levied each, amounting to $17.88. That was paid with a good deal of effort on the part of the parents of the offenders but it is a safe bet they not do the same thing again." *(Altoona Mirror)*

June 15, 1927: Notice— Party who stole tools from Thunder Lake fire tower is known and will avoid prosecution by returning same at once. Henry Friend, district ranger." *(Rhinelander Daily News)*

July 5, 1927: "Charles Kouse of East End, Altoona was given a hearing before Justice of the Peace John K. Shoenfelt of Duncansville, charged by the district fire warden with the defacing of state property at the Brush mountain [Blair County, Pennsylvania] fire tower, the latter part of last week. He was adjudged guilty of the charge and a fine of $10 with the costs of prosecution, was imposed. It was alleged that Kouse cut his name and other markings on the fire tower in violation of the law." *(The Altoona Mirror)*

March 27, 1928: "When the forest protectors opened the Fire Tower at gallows Hill in the town of Kingston [Ulster County, New York], a few days ago for the season, they found a number of broken windows in the observatory that had evidently been shot out by hunters. The State

Conservation Commission will impose a fine of $500 on the culprits if they can be detected." *(The Kingston Daily Freeman)*

April 19, 1928: "Deputy Sheriff William Gold recently stated that he has received a complaint from the forest ranger in charge of the McDade fire tower [Pennsylvania], on Mt. Jewett road near here, stating that the phone line running out of the place has been put out of commission several times by youths who climb the tower in his absence and slide horseshoes down the wire, wrecking it. The authorities believe that the youths have not realized the seriousness of their offense in rendering the tower useless in reporting fires, and state that if the mischief does not cease, prosecutions will follow.--Kane Republican." *(McKean Democrat)*

May 31, 1928: "A careless cigaret smoker is blamed for a fire which destroyed 200 acres of grass in the Boss ranch, seven miles east of here yesterday afternoon. The blaze was sighted from the Shuteye lookout station [Sierra National Forest, California], Fire Warden Jim Boutwell being notified. Recruiting 16 men Boutwell brought the flames under control late yesterday afternoon." *(Madera Tribune)*

October 8, 1928: "As part of a campaign to discourage visitors from writing or carving their names on property of the state bureau of forestry, eleven persons have been fined $2.50 by the commonwealth of Pennsylvania, according to an announcement made by W.L. Byers of McConnellsburg, district forester. [List of names and addresses] paid fines for disfiguring a fire tower on Blue Knob [Blue Knob State Park].

Because of the damage done to the Blue Knob tower, it has been decided that the lower two flights of steps will be removed from the tower when the towerman is not on duty. Mr. Bowers states that the department does not wish to deprive visitors of the benefit of the view, but that the loss in broken glass and locks and repairing woodwork has made the step necessary." *(Altoona Mirror)*

July 19, 1929: "State Forest Rangers were assisted by a crew from P.G.& E. Forebay Monday in extinguishing a fire which broke out along the pipe line below the El Dorado Power house. The blaze was discovered by the Leek Springs lookout [Eldorado National Forest, California] and is thought to have been started by careless smokers." *(The Mountain Democrat)*

August 1, 1929: "Punishment that fitted the crime was meted out to five caddy boys who damaged the state's fire tower on top of Whiteface Mountain [Essex County, New York]. These fire towers are favorite objectives for hikers and mountain climbers during the summer on account of the magnificent views obtainable from the glass enclosed rooms at the top. Thousands of visitors climb the towers every summer where they are always welcome and complaints of damage to the towers or meddling with the observer's instruments are practically unknown.

On July 10, the observer gave permission to the boys to visit the tower while he went down the mountain to bring up supplies. Upon his return he found that one of the four-light window sashes in the observation room was broken in the center.

Instead of prosecuting the boys, District Ranger James H. Hopkins of the conservation department told them that if they would buy a new sash and all five of them deliver it to the observer on the mountain he would call it square. Two days later the boys delivered the new sash and further proceedings were dropped. " *(The Adirondack Record-Elizabethtown News)*

May 1931: "The Prairie Mountain lookout house [Siuslaw National Forest) Western Lane Fire Patrol, Oregon] was broken into again this winter. A shutter from a south window had been removed and a glass broken out. The guest had remained long enough to use a gallon of kerosene and to get the dishes very dirty and things thoroughly messed up. Several things were taken from the house. Fortunately the visitor placed the shutter back over the broken window, otherwise things would have been badly damaged by the rain." *(The Salt* Forest newsletter*)*

October 17, 1931: "State police returned to Klamath Falls early today from Cruzette after an unsuccessful search for two unidentified men who attacked and beat Roy Beamer, forest lookout, after he found they had robbed his cabin. The police found abandoned bed rolls of the pair and tracked them into Box Canyon where they lost the trail.

Lieut. O.O. Nichols, of the state constabulary, and Deputy Sheriff Ross Brown left at noon for Crescent and the O'Dell country to continue the search [Wolf Mountain, Willamette National Forest, Oregon]." *(Roseburg News-Review)*

September 15, 1932: "Special measures to cope with the situation were taken when it was realized the fires were being set at night. A night shift was placed on Pike County Peak lookout [Plumas National Forest, California]." *(Feather River Bulletin)*

July 1, 1933: "Hugh Walker, district warden of Polk county, recently advised the State Forester that some individual had stolen the fire finder from the Bald Mountain lookout [Polk County FPA, Oregon]. While it was one of the old type and more or less obsolete, nevertheless, it served the purpose and the association will now have to provide another. Mr. Walker states that if there are any of the associations who have an extra one at the present time he would like to borrow it for awhile. At the same time he is wonderingg what use any one would have for a fire finder unless he is going to use it as a calling card when looking for a job as lookout. Associations are warned to be on the lookout for such a man." *(Forest Log)*

July 25, 1933: "Alpinists are blamed for extensive damage to the Bachelor Butte lookout station [Deschutes National Forest, Oregon]. The damage to the station consisted of a broken window. This, in turn admitted weather, pack rats and groundhogs to the station, constructed in 1931. Snow and rain warped and cupped the floor and the rats caused much damage.

Entry to the station is believed to have been made early this year

When the yet unknown party visited the station, the shutter was removed from one of the north windows, a central pane of glass was taken out and the window was opened. When the visitors left, the window, short one pane of glass, was fastened, but the shutter was not put in place. This left a vent for the weather and the rats. Alpine sticks were evidently used in prying open the shutter.

The gasoline stove and two kerosene heaters kept in the cabin were so badly rusted that they may be worthless. A survey of the damage was made yesterday by C.H. Overbay, Bend District Ranger. He made the trip to the summit with Harold Miller of Fall River and Darwin Clark, Bachelor Butte lookout." *(The Bend Bulletin)*

May 11, 1934: "Rangers at the Cheat View fire tower [West Virginia] said a man suspected of setting three fires had been trailed into Pennsylvania." *(Bluefield Daily Telegraph)*

July 1934: "Along toward the later part of May we had a spell of serious fire weather necessitating some emergency lookouts. When Ranger Wirth rushed a man up to Lookout Mountain [Ochoco National Forest] the telephone would not work. On investigation it was discovered that the brand new aluminum boxes containing the telephone lightning protection each had been shot into with a high powered rifle and that the contents were ruined. A search about the place revealed names of three men written on the lookout house along with the date of May 13. Also some rifle shells were found each bearing a peculiar scratch caused by the ejector. This constituted sufficient evidence for the State Police who were asked for assistance in handling the case.

Result— offenders hailed before the local court and relieved of $57.50. This should be a lesson to them and others who might be inclined to seek recreation at the expense of government property. H.C. Obye." *(Six Twenty-Six)*

🔥

July 5, 1935: "A small fire near the Truckee river between Boca and the Fly Casting club was put out yesterday by Frank Maher and other rangers from Martis peak lookout station. A small pump from Truckee was used. The fire was believed to have started from a fire made by fishermen on the bank of the river. Campers and fishermen were again warned yesterday by Maher to be careful in starting fires. A small patch of brush burned [Martis Peak, Tahoe National Forest, California]." *(Nevada State Journal)*

🔥

August 15, 1935: "The depredations of souvenir hunting tourists on Whiteface Mountain [Essex County, New York] has prompted the State Conservation department to adopt a set of regulations to end petty vandalism.

The new rules state that no person shall cut, remove or destroy any trees, timber, plants or flowers on certain state lands, nor shall any person leave rubbish thereon.

Department officials said persons climb to the fire observation tower at the summit, and then decide to carry off as a souvenir wild flowers, pieces of stone, moss or anything else that can be moved.

Officials feared that within a short time the entire mountain top would be denuded of any wild vegetables or floral growth and the new regulations were promulgated to forestall such a possibility." *(Adirondack Record-Elizabethtown Post)*

🔥

July 1937: "One of the worst examples of vandalism that has come to the attention of protection agencies for some time was the damage to the Saddle Mountain Lookout in Clatsop county [Oregon] some time during the past winter. Part of the fire finder, which had been left there, had disappeared and was probably thrown over the cliff. The stove suffered a like fate. The haze meter had the appearance of being damaged with a hammer. The telephone was in a similar condition. Only a few of the cooking utensils were left. The table, the cupboard, and all but one of the four chairs had been either chopped or broken to pieces. There was evidence of an attempted fire in one of the cupboards but it was evidently too wet to burn. The window blinds were ripped down and broken, the storm shutters were partially destroyed and the door completely missing. Winter storms had soaked everything remaining in the cabin. Not satisfied with confining their damage to the contents of the cabin, all windows were broken. Records and register of guests were partially destroyed. Protection officials have considerable evidence as to who the guilty parties are and it is believed that they will be apprehended." *(The Forest Log)*

April 1938: "For the second consecutive year vandals have been responsible for extensive damage to the Saddle Mountain Lookout [North Saddle Mountain, Oregon Department of Forestry/Clatsop FPA], located in Clatsop county District Warden H.C. Kyle, of Jewell, reports that 108 of the total of 116 small window panes in the building were broken and the furniture and interior damaged. State police were notified and several individuals held for questioning in regard to the damage but as yet no arrests have been made.

About the same time last year some individuals made a trip to the summit, broke out all the windows, tore down the storm shutters, threw the fire finder and stove over the cliff, ruined kitchen utensils and finally tried to set fire in one of the cupboards but evidently the material was too damp to burn. The guilty parties were never apprehended." *(The Forest Log)*

Saddle Mountain – *Clatsop County, Oregon*

June 11, 1934: Panorama photo taken by Robert Cooper.

April 1938: "The strong arm of Uncle Sam fell on Jack Warren of Fall Creek, Oregon, March 4, when, by jury trial in Justice of the Peace Bryson's court at Eugene, he was found guilty of possession of stolen Forest Service property. The stolen property was an electric lantern stamped U.S. Forest Service, which he evidently had taken from Eagle's Rest lookout house [Willamette National Forest] after gaining unlawful entrance some time during the fall of 1937." *(Six Twenty-Six)*

May 12, 1939: "Charles Cole of Onaway, a former fire tower guard for the state conservation department, was to be taken to state police headquarters at Lansing [Michigan] today for lie-detector tests in connection with investigation of the recent forest fire here.

Cole, questioned at Onaway by state police yesterday, denied any knowledge of the origin of the blaze which swept over 100,000 acres last week end.

Authorities suspect the fire was started by an incendiarist." *(Marshall Evening Chronicle)*

June 4, 1939: "Officers are investigating the destruction of a forest lookout tower on Wolf Mountain [Willamette National Forest, Oregon] three and a half miles above Cruzette and 20 miles east of Oakridge.

Some time during the past winter the tower, 65 feet high, crashed to the ground and was only discovered a few days ago on the first trip of forest employes to the mountain. It was found the turn buckle on one of the guy wires had been screwed off, allowing the tower to fall when a wind came up. It was a complete wreck, according to the officers." *(Eugene Register-Guard)*

September 29, 1939: "Charged with burglarizing the United States forest service Bald Eagle lookout in Boundary county, Leo Scott and Robert Montague of Sandpoint were arrested Wednesday by county and state officers, Sheriff Warren Rapp reported yesterday.

In a two page confession given Sheriff Rapp, the Sandpoint men admitted they stole a quantity of groceries from the lookout on September 14.

'We were searching for huckleberries in and around Bald Eagle mountain when it became dark and we sighted the lookout. We approached the lookout and observed the trap door was open. We then climbed the lookout and found that the outside door was off its hinges and that the inner door was open. We entered the lookout, secured a lunch from the foodstuffs found in the lookout, made up beds, using the blankets found in the lookout and went to bed,' the confession read.

'The next morning we secured our breakfast, took my packsack and a box found in the lookout and packed various articles including four wool blankets, alarm clock and one small first aid kit.' the confession said, listing many other items which they took.

They told the sheriff that they hid the articles at 417 S. Ella street in Sandpoint. 'We came back down town in Sandpoint and later returned to the house while no one was at home, when we took the articles and hid them between the walls of the house in the upstairs where the same were found by the arresting officers on the evening of September 27.'

The two men are being held on an open charge by the sheriff's office."
(Northern Idaho News)

December 14, 1939: "On complaint of Roy Studor, manager of the Forest Department of the Gould Paper Company at McKeever [Herkimer County, New York], Trooper G.B. Vaughn entered the wilderness in search of a person who had cut about 75 feet of telephone wire connecting the McKeever office with the company's camps and the tower at Woodhull Mountain.

The cut was found back in the woods about three miles, in the vicinity of Remson Falls. Trooper Vaughn made an investigation and learned that the work had been done by Frankwayne Bodley, 21, of Chitteango, who said he needed the wire to erect his tent. Charged with malicious mischief he pleaded guilty and forfeited a fine of $25." *(Adirondack Record-Elizabethtown Post)*

Woodhull Mountain

Herkimer County, New York

1917

New York State Archives

Bald Knob

Siskiyou National

Forest, Oregon

September 21, 2008

Ron Kemnow Photo

May 1940: "Position covers lightning area in Port Orford district [Siskiyou National Forest, Oregon], and the area north of Agness in which several man-caused fires have occurred. The seen area in the Agness district justifies the manning of this point early in the year. In past years the position has been manned much earlier than the suggested opening date, while the existing opening date is so far out of line with actual needs that it has not been observed." *(Plans, Guard Placement, Siskiyou National Forest)*

August 1, 1940: "Two fires caused by careless smokers occurred Sunday, July 28, on the Klamath Reservation. One about a mile northwest of Modoc Point Lookout [Klamath Indian Agency/Winema National Forest, Oregon] was controlled by grazing permitees and Indian Service officers before it got under way." *(Chiloquin Review)*

September 14, 1940: "Apparently started by hunters in a cove near Marshall boulevard and Mt. Vernon avenue, a brush fire swept to the summit of Little Mountain [San Bernardino County/California Department of Forestry] yesterday afternoon, threatening the state forest service lookout station.

The blaze was brought under control after about two hours, with but little damage. Foresters estimated that the fire burned approximately 150 acres of brush.

Crews directed by State Ranger Russell Z. Smith managed to save the lookout station." *(The San Bernardino County Sun)*

July 4, 1941: The first forest fire reported in this area resulting from the careless use of fireworks was reported Wednesday by officials of Mono National Forest.

More than 400 square feet of forest land was burned over near Zephyr Cove, Lake Tahoe [Nevada]. Forest Rangers reported the blaze originated from the careless use of firecrackers.

Discovered by residents of the resort area, the blaze was reported to the forest service. Jim Cain, Douglas county fire warden at Zephyr Point lookout station, took charge of suppression measures. The Zephyr Point forest service pumper was pressed into service." *(Nevada State Journal)*

July 24, 1941: "The United States forestry man at Black mountain lookout station [San Bernardino National Forest, California] discovered a man through his powerful glasses setting fire to brush and weeds along the highway early Monday morning.

The lookout called the sheriff's department at Riverside and the news was dispatched to Banning quickly. Deputy Sheriff Claude McCracken and State Traffic Officers Doyle Jessup and Charles Gandy hurried to Cabazon to see if they could apprehend the culprit. The lookout man saw him get out of his car, light several fires and return quickly to the car and drive away.

The state fire truck also was sent to the scene of the fires, which they readily extinguished. So far the guilty person has not been located." *(The San Bernardino County Sun)*

January 19, 1943: "The Mt. Noorat Lookout [Victoria, Australia] which warns bush fire brigades for miles around of outbreaks of fire, was, while closed for the winter, badly damaged by vandals.

Reporting this to the annual conference of district brigades, in Camperdown last week, the secretary of the Noorat brigade (Mr G. Webb) said the damage looked more like the work of irresponsible men than of children. The door had been taken off and thrown down the crater and the telephone smashed. This meant borrowing a telephone at the beginning of this summer, until one could be procured by the P.M.G.

Delegates who know the value of the Lookout, described this vandalism as "deplorable." *(Camperdown Chronicle)*

December 29, 1946: "Vandals have been causing considerable destruction of government property in the park area on the summit of Mary's peak [Oregon], according to Siuslaw National Forest Supervisor Fred Furst, and unless the practice is curbed it may become necessary to close the road leading to the top except at times when guards are on duty in the park area.

Furst said most of the damage had been done with guns and consisted mostly in wanton shooting out of windows in rest rooms and in the forest lookout station. Broken windows in the lookout have allowed rain and snow to enter, warping the floor. Twenty-three out of 30 windowpanes in one rest room have been shot out and the initials F.G. shot into the walls. All water faucets from the water system in the camping area have been stolen." *(The Sunday Oregonian)*

August 15, 1947: "Green Peak State Forestry Lookout [Oregon] short wave radio was stolen Sunday night from the lookout tower while Anthony Kelly, lookout, slept in the cabin some 300 yards away. The vandals gained entrance to the tower through a window.

State police and state forestry officials investigating the crime found sufficient finger prints, tire tracks and other clues which may lead to an early arrest.

Loss of the two-way radio, the only means of communication with the lookout, has seriously jeopardized the surrounding area for lookout coverage and fire reports.

The small portable radio is plainly marked by the state forestry department and is licensed by the Federal Communications Commission. Misuse and tampering with such radios becomes a federal offense with heavy penalties in federal courts.

Should the radio be abandoned by the thieves, or any information regarding it, report should be made immediately to the state forestry office, Dallas 222, collect, or the state police." *(Corvallis Gazette-Times)*

August 23, 1948: "Ten Boy Scouts climbed Bachelor Butte [Deschutes National Forest, Oregon] Saturday. Evidence of vandalism was found at the summit, they said, where windows of the lookout station had been broken, and garbage was strewn about." *(The Bend Bulletin)*

August 25, 1948: "Between 75 and 80 men battled Tuesday night to control a fire 25 miles south of Deadwood and Lead in the Black Hills National Forest [South Dakota] on the highest fire danger day of the season.

The fire was believed to have been caused by a cigarette carelessly tossed along the road. It was definitely man-caused. It was under control by 10:30 p.m.

It was discovered by Wesley Groshong, emergency lookout at the Veterans Tower near Sturgis, who relayed its location to Custer town lookout. Ranger Orlo Jackson, Nemo, who was in Deadwood, left immediately for the fire. *(Deadwood Pioneer-Times)*

July 11, 1949: "Ray Antley on Lookout Butte [Rogue River National Forest/Winema National Forest, Oregon] with Rex Morehouse and two men from the Lake of the Woods fire suppression crew fought a fire which had apparently been started by a cigarette and burned one-half acre of lodgepole pine before it was brought under control." *(Herald and News)*

September 29, 1949: "Figuring himself lost in the wilds of the Plumas National Forest, D.J. Costa, a 21-year-old hunter from Chico, set the forest on fire at the edge of a logging road and within three miles of Lights Creek Ranger Station shortly before noon on September 25. Panic stricken, and facing the thought of a possible night alone in the woods with wild animals prowling around him, left it to attempt a return to camp. He was overjoyed when meeting Sid Donathan, forest fireman who had been dispatched to investigate Costa's fire which had been spotted by nearby Red Rock Lookout [Plumas National Forest, California]. Readily admitting he had set the fire in his fear of being lost, Costa was charged with negligence for having caused a forest fire.

Taken before Justice of the Peace Frank Standart of Greenville, Costa was fined $25, with $15 of the amount suspended." *(Indian Valley Record)*

August 7, 1950: "An abandoned camp fire was blamed for the more serious of two fires which had started up Davis Mountain from the east shore of Davis lake. The fire was spotted and brought under control by Tom Morris, Davis mountain lookout [Deschutes National Forest, Oregon]. The fire threatened a stand of marketable pine timber and was confined to less than an acre." *(The Bend Bulletin)*

Red Rock

Plumas National Forest, California

September 2008 – Ron Kemnow Photo

October 12, 1950: "Burglars broke into the Hardscrabble lookout station [Ochoco National Forest, Oregon] in the Ochoco National forest 75 miles east of Prineville, it was reported Monday by Joe Thalhofer, administrative assistant in the forest staff. Two lanterns were stolen, he said. State police were asked to investigate.

Rangers were asked to check on other lookout stations for possible burglaries. The Hardscrabble station was believed to have been entered by hunters who took the lanterns for their camps." *(Central Oregonian)*

October 19, 1950: "Forest service officials as well as private individuals have complained of the destructiveness of some sportsmen.

Rocky Top lookout [Oregon Department of Forestry/Clackamas-Marion FPA, Marion County], which is federal property and padlocked, was entered by a group of local hunters, who found it a convenient and dry camp.

This is the second year that this lookout has been used by deer hunters. Still remembered by forest representatives, was the fact that dry wood stored in the lookout was used freely last year. The wood was carried up hill a quarter mile in armloads by Arnold Sipe, the lookout. Pack rats had also entered the hole made by the intruders and caused considerable damage.

Keith Phillips, fire warden states that lookout stations are state and federal property, not to be used except in case of emergency." *(The Oregon Statesman)*

Rocky Top

Marion County

Oregon

1949 – Oregon Department of Forestry Photo

December 11, 1950: "Wise County Forest Warden Owen C. Carter reports that the Buck Knob tower building [Virginia] was broken into a few nights ago by unknown parties who carried off several cans of carbide and some groceries which had been stored there by the tender. None of the fire-fighting equipment had been molested. This is the second time this tower has been entered. Some months ago it was broken into and practically everything it contained was stolen or destroyed." *(Middlesboro Daily News - Kentucky)*

January 4, 1951: "Florida Forest rangers today are investigating several woods fires that burned hundreds of acres of valuable woodlands near Vicksburg fire tower [Bay County, Florida] on the Chipley highway last night, the officers reported today.

Officials of the Bay county station located on West 15th street, said there was evidence that the fires were deliberately set. Rangers battled the blaze for several hours before rainfall in the area helped extinguish the fires, the official reported." *(Panama City News-Herald)*

November 2, 1951: "Four Pen Mar youths are in the Franklin County, Pa. jail pending investigation of a series of thefts in the mountain area recently.

Three of the boys— two of whom are 16 and the other two 17— have admitted to police they stole gasoline from the property of R.G. Happel last

Sunday and also entered the cottage of the Forestry Department towerman at Mt. Dunlap last week." *(The Morning Herald)*

July 21, 1952: "Two minor forest fires occurred in this district over the weekend and both were extinguished without damage, it was reported today. Saturday a small area was burned over in the Snow creek region. This fire, apparently started by a fisherman, was spotted by the Round mountain lookout [Deschutes National Forest, Oregon]." *(The Bend Bulletin)*

July 23, 1953: "Vandalism has reached a new high here— 75 feet to be exact.

Forest fire tower observer Ariel Mowry told police that when she reported for work yesterday she found windows broken and rocks on the floor of the lofty observation post [Woonsocket, Providence County, Rhode Island]." *(The Zanesville Signal* - Ohio*)*

June 1, 1954: "Arrowhead hunters in the Geneva area of Jefferson county, west of the Deschutes gorge, were blamed for a fire earlier last week that was controlled by men from the Central Oregon state district office in Sisters. The fire was spotted by the Henkle butte lookout [Deschutes County, Oregon]. The blaze was small." *(The Bend Bulletin)*

January 5, 1955: "Forestry officers in Bendigo are asking the public to help them by reporting people who dump rubbish in forest areas.

A few hundred feet below the firewatchers' lookout on One Tree Hill [North West District, Victoria, Australia] near Bendigo, a dump of old clothing, newspapers, tins, and broken glass has been discovered.

The dump is close to a road leading to the lookout, which hundreds of people visit each year to get a 50-miles all-round glimpse of the countryside.

The forestry officers say the dumps are a grave fire risk in the summer, apart from marring the beauty of the spots around the city

They are still watching a huge dump of feathers in forest country near Junortoun, which caught fire last Friday.

Although the blaze was promptly put out, it is feared the feathers might burst into flame again and start a bush fire.

So far the Commission has been unable to find the culprit." *(The Argus)*

February 12, 1955: "Someone shot off the lock, broke two windows and stole several items from the Capital Peak lookout station of the State Department of Forestry [Washington]. Two sleeping bags and a supply of C-rations were taken by burglars who entered the ground-level house of the lookout station.

Max Gulberson told sheriff's deputies the burglary occurred sometime between January 25 and Wednesday, when it was discovered." *(The Daily Chronicle)*

August 8, 1956: "Quick action by several crews of trained forest fire fighters brought a potentially dangerous fire at the peak of Frazier mountain [Los Padres National Forest, California] under control yesterday with loss of only 50 acres of pine and brush.

Pinos Forest district ranger Tom Neff praised quick reporting by Frazier Mountain Lookout Lee Hartley.

Carelessness of one or more deer hunters was blamed for the blaze." *(Santa Cruz Sentinel)*

October 26, 1956: "Vandals have caused several hundred dollars damage to the fire tower and cabin on Bald Eagle mountain, north of Tyrone [Pennsylvania], district forestry officials reported this week.

Neal Carstetter, district inspector, said damage included broken windows, hatchet slashes in tower trap door, dumping fire-fighting tools and equipment into cistern, theft of door latches and breaking of lamps.

Mr. Carstetter said the almost exact hour of the incident took place has been determined and the perpetrators face heavy penalties when caught." *(The Altoona Mirror)*

November 1956: "A short time ago Dennis Mawhirter, Pittsburg, assistant district warden for the Columbia county unit of the Northwest State district, had occasion to make a trip to the Baker Point lookout [Columbia County, Oregon] and found that the locks had been broken off the station and the remote unit of the radio installation stolen.

While calling to report the theft to the Forest Grove office, another call came in from a radio shop in Cornelius saying that two juveniles had brought a piece of the state forestry department radio equipment into the shop to be repaired. The state license was still inside the unit.

The two youngsters said there was a man with them at the time the equipment was stolen but they did not know his name. The state police are on his trail." *(The Forest Log)*

December 6, 1956: "Conservation Department forest fire lookouts, kept busy by fires, low-flying planes, heavy winds and severe electrical storms, ran into another threat during hunting seasons this fall.

Lookouts Medford Moore and Rieno Narva, seasoned veterans of the Traverse City district fire detection system, were unwilling observers of wild shooting near their towers.

Moore reported that a man and a boy came out of the woods near his tower in Fife Lake state forest [Michigan] and set up a target on a nearby rock. While the two were shooting, a slug glanced off the rock and hit the tower cab. Before Moore could say a word the pair beat a hasty retreat into the woods." *Clare Sentinel)*

1956: Two window panes were replaced after being broken out by vandals [South Saddle Mountain, Tillamook Fire Patrol, Oregon, Washington County].

September 16, 1958: "So far, there have been no bad fires in the Hills this summer. A[lk man-caused fire started near Pactola Reservoir two weeks ago, but burned only two acres.

The fire was spotted by the Boulder Hill Lookout [Black Hills National Forest, South Dakota], and farmers, ranchers and others fought it out with gunny sacks and

September 28, 1958: "State police of the Tupper Lake [St. Lawrence County, New York] sub-station investigating a case of destructive vandalism reported Sept. 14, cleared up that case Saturday and with it two others.

The names of the two Piercefield boys are withheld because of their age, 8 and 10 years. The damage will run into hundreds of dollars.

The names of the two Piercefield boys are withheld because of their age, 8 and 10 years. The damage will run into hundreds of dollars.

The first complaint on Sept. 14 came from George LaVasseur, Piercefield, fire warden on nearby Mt. Arab who reported that the state-owned observer's cabin on the mountain had been broken into and damaged Two rifles, an 8-mm Mauser and a single-shot .22, and two revolvers, a P-38 Luger and a .45 Colt, were taken from a gun cabinet, loaded with ammunition found on the premises, and repeatedly fired. In 'shooting up'

La Vaughn Vanderburg Kemnow

the cabin the intruders shattered a barometer, thermometer and other equipment and furnishings. They then moved out on the cabin porch and used the fire tower for a target, they ruined the roof." **(Advance-News)**

Boulder Hill

Black Hills National Forest, South Dakota

June 26, 1939 – National Archives

October 12, 1958: "About 60 forest fires, apparently the work of arsonists, broke out Saturday in Taylor County.

A spokesman for the State Forestry Service said the telephone line from the Salem fire tower in Taylor County was cut.

An estimated 500 to 1,000 acres of woodlands were burning, all in the southwest part of the county near Gulf coast.

The forestry service spokesman said that none of the fires was near dwellings. Forestry service workers were moved in from several adjoining counties and firefighters in other parts of the state were alerted to furnish aid if it proved necessary. Private landowners, including the Buckeye Cellulose Co. with extensive landholdings in the area, also lent aid." *(The Evening Independent)*

October 19, 1959: "One fire, a 200-acre blaze in Halley Canyon, definitely was set, the U.S. Forest Service said. Officials said a lookout in the Whitaker Peak station [Angeles National Forest, California] saw a man drive up, set the fire, and drive away.

About an hour later, 10 miles from Halley Canyon blaze, another small fire began, and officials said it looked like arson. It had burned about 200 acres.

The third blaze, on Whitaker Peak, finally forced the evacuation of the lookout tower. That blaze charred 100 acres." *(The Arizona Republic)*

Whittaker Peak

Angeles National

Forest, California

1940

National Archives

1959: The new 3-story lookout house [Aldrich Mountain, Grant County, Oregon] was destroyed when vandals burned it down later in the year.

28 — La Vaughn Vanderburg Kemnow

September 28, 1958: "State police of the Tupper Lake [St. Lawrence County, New York] sub-station investigating a case of destructive vandalism reported Sept. 14, cleared up that case Saturday and with it two others.

October 12, 1958: "About 60 forest fires, apparently the work of arsonists, broke out Saturday in Taylor County.

A spokesman for the State Forestry Service said the telephone line from the Salem fire tower in Taylor County was cut.

An estimated 500 to 1,000 acres of woodlands were burning, all in the southwest part of the county near Gulf coast.

The forestry service spokesman said that none of the fires was near dwellings. Forestry service workers were moved in from several adjoining counties and firefighters in other parts of the state were alerted to furnish aid if it proved necessary. Private landowners, including the Buckeye Cellulose Co. with extensive landholdings in the area, also lent aid." *(The Evening Independent)*

October 19, 1959: "One fire, a 200-acre blaze in Halley Canyon, definitely was set, the U.S. Forest Service said. Officials said a lookout in the Whitaker Peak station [Angeles National Forest, California] saw a man drive up, set the fire, and drive away.

About an hour later, 10 miles from Halley Canyon blaze, another small fire began, and officials said it looked like arson. It had burned about 200 acres.

The third blaze, on Whitaker Peak, finally forced the evacuation of the lookout tower. That blaze charred 100 acres." *(The Arizona Republic)*

1959: The new 3-story lookout house [Aldrich Mountain, Grant County, Oregon] was destroyed when vandals burned it down later in the year.

September 28, 1960: "Lewis county sheriff's officers said Wednesday they are investigating the breakin of the Doty [State Department of Forestry, Washington] forest lookout sometime early this week. Boards were knocked off of the lookout tower and a radio antenna pole ripped down. All 10 big windows in a bunkhouse were broken. The lookout station is operated during the summer fire season by the Chehalis headquarters of the State Department of Natural Resources." *(The Daily Chronicle)*

Whittaker Peak

Angeles National

Forest, California

1940

National Archives

1959: The new 3-story lookout house [Aldrich Mountain, Grant County, Oregon] was destroyed when vandals burned it down later in the year.

🔺

September 28, 1960: "Lewis county sheriff's officers said Wednesday they are investigating the breakin of the Doty [State Department of Forestry, Washington] forest lookout sometime early this week. Boards were knocked off of the lookout tower and a radio antenna pole ripped down. All 10 big windows in a bunkhouse were broken. The lookout station is operated during the summer fire season by the Chehalis headquarters of the State Department of Natural Resources." *(The Daily Chronicle)*

🔺

October 18, 1961: "Three persons waved preliminary hearing and were bound over to the grand jury Tuesday on a charge of theft of property from a government lookout station on Larch Mountain [Mt. Hood National Forest, Oregon]." *(The Oregonian)*

🔺

April 25, 1962: "When John Sloss, Deadwood, opened up Custer Peak fire lookout for the Black Hills National Forest [South Dakota] Tuesday he found that the station had been broken into during the winter months while it was closed.

The break-in was apparently quite recent, Charles Hathaway, district ranger said. A further investigation is being made. Sloss went on temporary duty at the lookout Tuesday because of the fire hazard brought on by drought and warm weather." *(Lead Daily Call)*

June 7, 1962: "Careless picnickers were responsible for a fire at Sly Park last Monday that destroyed over a quarter of an acre of brush and damaged many pine trees in the recreation area.

Despite the fact that fires are not permitted in the recreation area outside the designated camp grounds, campers have ignored the posted regulations.

The fire was spotted from the Baltic Lookout station [Eldorado National Forest & California Department of Forestry] by Mrs. Eula Mae Nevins, and resulted in CDF crews arriving at the park shortly after noon, where they found fishermen in the area attempting to put the fire out.

Assistant ranger, Vernon Stahl, stated that the fire hazard in the Sly Park area is serious, especially when campers will not cooperate with fire rules of the area. Strict enforcement of the fire regulations will be carried out in the area hereafter, Stahl said." *(The Mountain Democrat and Placerville Times)*

1962: Some one climbed to the catwalk and shot through the building shutters about center height of the windows, hitting the stove pipe and damper on the way through [Snowboard Ridge, Oregon Department of Forestry, Wheeler County].

May 23, 1963: Vandals recently did $120 worth of damage to the Hogback Mountain lookout station. According to "George Wardell, KFPA supervisor, "the miscreants stood outside the tower and discharged their rifles up through the floor of the station." They also burned down the restroom, broke into the tower, and threw various items onto the ground. This is reported to be the third time vandals have ravaged the lookout since last winter. *(Herald and News)*

May 23, 1963: "Vandalism of the Hogback Mountain lookout station [Klamath FPA, Klamath County, Oregon] sometime last weekend has been estimated at more than $120 in damage, the KFPA reported Thursday.

It was the third time since last winter that quarters of the KFPA have been the subject of vandalism, according to George Wardell, supervisor of the association.

Wardell said that the miscreants stood outside the tower and discharged their rifles up through the floor of the station.

They also tore a hand railing and a number of steps from the building, burned down the restroom nearby, and broke into the tower, where they picked up various items and threw them onto the ground below.

A crew has been assigned to repair damage to the lookout, Wardell said. "
(Herald and News)

Larch Mountain
Mount Hood National Forest, Oregon
No Date – Trails Club of Oregon Archives

June 16, 1963: "Authorities sounded a statewide alert Saturday for a steel-bed tractor hauler stolen from the Moselle fire tower near here (Hattiesburg) [Mississippi]." *(Monroe Morning World)*

August 16, 1963: "Winema Forest Ranger Reports Wide Spread Vandalism In The Woods:

"The first episode developed several weeks ago when someone clipped the wires connecting a telephone receiver to an emergency telephone box near the summer homes on the east side of Lake of the Woods.

The telephone linked that area with the fire lookout station at Buck Peak [Rogue River National Forest›Klamath Forest Protective Association›Winema National Forest, Oregon] and the Lake of the Woods. When the receiver was disconnected from the telephone the residents of that vicinity were deprived of the only means of communication to report a fire.

In addition, communications between Buck Peak and the ranger station were disrupted. The severing of the wires had "opened the three phone circuit" and the lookout could not contact the ranger station, although the latter could call the guard tower.

If at that time a fire had broken out in the region under surveillance by Buck Peak lookout, that guard would have been unable to report it to the fire control officer at Lake of the Woods. Several days after the wire cutting, employees of the district traced the disruption of telephone service to the telephone east of the lake.

Meanwhile, an electrical storm had blown into the Winema Forest with the result that lightning started fires in the vicinity of Buck Peak. Dispatchers for the district were required to keep in constant contact with the lookout because there was no efficient method for him to call headquarters.

The remaining incident was in the form of four fires which had been set intentionally along a forest access road, about 10 miles south of Lake of the Woods, near Buck Peak, last Sunday. *"(Herald and News - By Dick Biggs)*

October 12, 1963: "Eager hunters determined on vandalism went all the way to the top of a mountain to the Doty Lookout station [State Department of Forestry, Lewis County, Washington] to tip over the outhouse and throw it in the brush 15 feet from the open hole. This is senseless destruction.

Mutilated signs for the protection of life and property do little good when hunters shoot at them for target practice. Robert Joyce, assistant district administrator, Chehalis, examines (photo) a sign full of holes on the Doty Lookout." *(The Daily Chronicle)*

June 19, 1964: "The destruction of the Doty Lookout [State Department of Forestry, Lewis County Washington] by vandals sometime during the past two months has left the fire lookout tower 'in a mess,' Wayne Johnson, Chehalis district administrator, State Department of Natural Resources, reported Friday

'We went up this week to ready the post for the summer fire season before a lookout is stationed there and found the shelter in a mess,' Johnson said.

The heavy duty cable that is wrapped around the tower to protect the shutters was removed and stolen. Entry to the post was made by forcing the door. Thirty windows in the tower were smashed. Some were shot out and others broken with rocks or poked through with sticks. A grill on a stove was ripped out and stolen.

In addition, 80 feet of lightning arrester cable on the tower legs was stolen and 20 feet of copper tubing taken.

'The tower is subject to vandalism every year, but this year was the worst,' Johnson said." *(The Daily Chronicle)*

June 27, 1964: "Vandals recently climbed the Glover Lake fire tower in Manistee county [Michigan] and dropped large rocks from the tower, breaking wooden steps and actually bending the iron tower supports. Broken beer bottles were strewn over the area below the tower." *(Record-Eagle)*

October 29, 1964: "George Bice, fire control assistant on the Long Creek ranger district of the Malheur national forest [Oregon], reports that some flagrant vandalism occurred on the district over the weekend

While the lookout at Lake Butte was temporarily absent from the lookout tower Saturday morning, several shots were fired through the lookout post. There is considered no chance that the shots were accidental, because at least three bullets were fired directly upward through the floor and others were put through window casings. Repairs of the damage will be expensive because it will be necessary not only to patch the holes but to re-lay the tile flooring.

State police are investigating and have in their possession both bullets and empty cartridge cases. Bice points out that the culprits, if apprehended, can be tried in either state or federal court, since vandalism is a state offense and damaging government property is a federal offense." *(Blue Mountain Eagle)*

1965: A 30-foot steel tower erected, a portable cab that broke down into sections for removal during the off season due to a constant high occurrence of vandalism [Lookout Mountain, Oregon Department of Forestry, Clackamas-Marion FPA].

Lake Butte

Malheur National Forest

Oregon

1963

Malheur National Forest

Archives

September 1966: With apprehension of six teenage boys, a severe case of vandalism at Deans Mountain Lookout within the Coos Forest Protective Association, was cleared up recently.

Damage to the station was extensive. It had been shot up and besmeared with paint. Ernie Labart, forest warden 2, at Reedsport first got a lead on the boys and then, through the investigation of Norris Joyce, chief investigator for the department who was ably assisted by Labart, the boys were brought to justice. Several days were consumed in the process.

A confession was obtained from one, who in turn, implicated the others.

They were bound over to justice court." *(The Forest Log)*

🔥

April 26, 1967: "Tom Goodrich, a Forest Service ranger from Arizona said, "As near as we can tell the fire was started by man. There were no lightning strikes reported Tuesday night and that's the best guess."

The FBI and Forest Service are carrying out an intensive investigation, he said.

Besides the lush timber, the only property damage reported was the Forest Service's Sacramento Lookout Tower about five miles southeast of the community of Sunspot." *(Albuquerque Tribune)*

↟

January 23, 1968: "The sheriff's office was notified Monday of the burglary of a lookout tower at Mount Pleasant [*Washington Department of Natural Resources*]. There was no report on what was stolen." *(Port Angeles Evening News)*

↟

1968: "The copper wire used as lightning protection was stolen. Investigation of this was made in co-operation with the Oregon State Police. The guilty party was apprehended and tried in District Court. He was convicted and placed on probation subject to making restitution of the value of the stolen property [Castle Rock (Bear Mountain), Eastern Lane Division, Oregon Department of Forestry]." *(Eastern Lane District Annual Report)*

↟

July 14, 1969: "The Stratton fire tower [Green Mountain National Forest, Vermont] is practically never bothered by vandals during the hiking season, but every spring, all the windows have to be replaced and the accumulation of beer cans and bottles left by the skiers cleaned out. The ski lift makes it easily accessible to crowds, and hence vulnerable." *(Berkshire Eagle* Mass.*)*

↟

1969: "During the 1969 hunting season the tower on Baughman [Douglas County, Oregon] sustained extensive damage that must be repaired before it can be used." *(Douglas FPA - Oregon Department of Forestry Annual Report - 1969)*

↟

1969: The lookout was burned by an arsonist [Logger Butte, Willamette National Forest, Oregon].

↟

March 4, 1970: "Thorn Lookout Station near Dayton, Washington, Umatilla National Forest, was broken into three times. Damage to the structure, maintained cooperatively with the Washington State Department of Natural Resources, and the value of articles was estimated at $460." *(Port Angeles Evening News)*

↟

November 30, 1970: Wood County police on routine patrol early Sunday morning reported that a 60-foot fire lookout tower located on a hill near the Wood-Adams County line had apparently been blown down.

The tower, owned by Nekoosa-Edwards Paper Co., was used mainly as an auxiliary tower for the past several years, and had not been manned on a regular basis.

Police are investigating the possibility that someone may have removed some support bolts at the base of the tower." *(The Daily Tribune)*

1970: "All window glass had to be replaced in Baughman Lookout [Douglas County, Oregon] because of vandalism." *(Douglas FPA - Oregon Department of Forestry Annual Report - 1970)*

November 1970: "During the past grouse season, 'brave' persons unknown attacked the Glass Hill lookout station [Oregon Department of Forestry, Union County] in Northeast Oregon District. Casualties counted were nine windows and a couple padlocks." *(Forest Log)*

1971: Roundtop Lookout was checked on May 10 to assess winter damage, if any. On the morning of May 18, Tom Davis and Paulo Sparks returned to the lookout to do maintenance work. The following vandalism has occurred since May 10: Forced entry through the door, stole one, 2 ½-pound dry chemical fire extinguisher, one LPG light, one LPG Astrol 'A' refer and twelve feet of 3/16-inch copper tubing. Estimated cost to replace and repair is $213.00.

June 10, 1972: "Charles Wilda, charged with toppling a fire lookout tower and trying to topple another tower last fall, was found innocent Friday by reason of insanity.

Lincoln County Court Judge Donald Schnabel said he based his ruling on psychiatric examinations conducted after Wilda, 29, of Whitelaw, entered his plea April 12 of innocent by reason of insanity.

Wilda had been named in six counts, including criminal damage to property, in the toppling of Natural Resources fire lookout tower Nov. 5.

He also was accused of attempted criminal damage to property in the removal of bolts from an AT&T microwave tower the same day.

Both towers were on Lookout Mountain in Lincoln County [Wisconsin]. *(The Milwaukee Sentinel)*

November 15, 1973: "Gerry Traver is an observer for the State Department of Environmental Conservation stationed at the Stissing Mountain tower

[Delaware county, New York]. The tower was reactivated in July of this year and it commands a spectacular view of the surrounding countryside.

In the time since the Stissing tower was closed there has been considerable damage caused by unknown people visiting the top of the peak. A cabin at the tower's base had been broken into. Floor joists under the porch had been chopped at, windows were broken and boards had been ripped off. Someone had also broken into the tower observatory. The old door had been chopped through and floor boards were cut. Only recently the observer's out house was pushed off its foundation. Since the station was opened, Observer Traver and District Ranger Richard Swanson have kept close watch on the station." *(The Register-Herald)*

December 18, 1973: "Carl P. Shultz of Swain Groves reported that the house located at the Adams Fire Tower [Florida], west of Fort Pierce, had been broken into and several household items were taken." *(The News Tribune)*

January 16, 1974: "Six juveniles from the Coibleskill area were arrested late Sunday for allegedly breaking into the communications center at the Petersburg fire tower in Schoharie County.

The fire tower was purchased last year by the Schoharie County government for $10, to be used by the Schoharie County Amateur Radio group. The radio group provides communications for the county in cases of emergencies and has since complained of vandalism at the tower which they had renovated to serve their purpose.

The six youths, ranging from age 16 to 17, were arrested by Trooper Pat Donnelly of the Warnerville State Police substation in connection with a break-in at the tower Friday. They were arraigned before Justice Merton Utter of Richmondville and were released in the custody of their parents waiting further court action." *(Schenectady Gazette)*

May 17, 1974: "Extensive damage was done to the KFPA Hogback Mountain lookout [Klamath County, Oregon] in what was termed 'the worst incident of malicious damage we've ever had.'

According to Bud Van Hoy, KFPA assistant district forester, between $1400 and $1500 worth of damage was done in the past two weeks at the lookout located near the old Oregon Tech campus.

All windows were broken while stoves, furniture, bedding and 'anything loose or which could be pulled loose' was thrown from the lookout.

Repairs are expected to take about two weeks. Besides property damages, Van Hoy estimated labor costs for repairs will also run between $1400 and $1500. Damages were discovered by a radio equipment inspector earlier this week but KFPA was not informed until Thursday." (*Herald and News*)

October 31, 1974: The lookout was burned by vandals [Castle Rock, Willamette National Forest, Oregon].

1974: "All the glass was broken out of the tower [Lowell Butte, Eastern Lane District, Oregon Department of Forestry]. Instead of replacing with glass, we used large sheets of 3/16" plexiglass, this allowed removal at the end of the fire season and ¼" plywood was used to keep out the winter weather. The living quarters also received 15 to 20 broken windows. The wood cook stove was stolen one week previous to occupancy by the lookout. This was replaced with a gas cook stove which was removed at the end of fire season." (*Eastern Lane District Annual Report*)

June 10, 1976: "Vandals have again been at work damaging and destroying public property on the Gauley Ranger District of the Monogahela National Forest The Red Oak Fire Tower [Webster County, West Virginia] which has been maintained for emergency fire detection and forest communication throughout the Cranberry Back Country and Wilderness Study Area and for use by the W. Va. DNR in their bear tracking program has just recently received such unwarranted destruction.

The electrical service box and wiring have been torn out and damaged beyond repair with the cabin's interior electrical heaters stolen. Locks have been broken to gain entry to the tower cabin with contents of the cabin thrown about. The tower was to have been in use as a communication post during the National Girl Scout Encampment to be held here in Mid June." (*The Pocahontas Times*)

July 15, 1976: "Some recent examples of vandalism occurring are removal of a propane tank regulator and all copper tubing at Indian Rock Lookout [Malheur National Forest, Oregon]." (*Blue Mountain* **Eagle**)

Indian Rock
Malheur

National

Forest Oregon

2008

Ron Kemnow

Photo

July 15, 1976: "The last half mile of Pilot Peak Road off of LaPorte Rd. at Onion Valley on Plumas National Forest [California] will be gated to restrict vehicle access to the new lookout construction site," said Lloyd R. Britton, Plumas National Forest Supervisor.

'This administrative action has been taken to reduce the chance of further vandalism to the construction project' added Britton.

The new lookout building is being constructed to replace the previous one which was burned down by vandals. Completion expected by Oct. with use scheduled for next year.

The gate will be located so as not to interfere with any uses other than that of the road itself, Britton said.

The road will be reopened when the lookout is completed." *(Feather River Bulletin)*

🔥

October 21, 1976: "Recent damages to the Red Oak fire tower [Webster County, West Virginia] by vandals on the Gauley Ranger District, Monogahela National Forest is estimated at $700.00. Electrical service boxes and lines have been torn out, interior contents and fire detection equipment have been damaged and one of the special large pane windows has been broken out.

The Red Oak fire tower has been repeatedly damaged by vandals over the past year. The Army Corp of Engineers who operates a remote flood control station at the tower site recently had $2,500 of flood monitoring equipment removed from the site.

Anyone observing or having information concerning such acts of vandalism are asked to contact the nearest law enforcement authority or U.S. Forest Ranger Station." *(The Pocahontas Times)*

🔥

1976-77: The lookout was burned by vandals [Ventana Double Cone, Los Padres National Forest, Californial. *(Lookouts of the Los Padres Forest* - By Irma Oksen Reaves*)*

⛰️

June 26, 1977: "The fire's source was reportedly an illegal campfire on a U.S. Forest Service tree farm in the upper Big Tujunga Canyon area, according to Pat Pontes of the Forest Service. Pontes said investigators knew who was responsible for the campfire.

The only structures threatened were the lookout station on Vetter Peak [Angeles National Forest, Californial and Southern California Edison power lines running across the area, Pontes said." *(Star-News)*

⛰️

June 1, 1978: "Dry Soda Lookout [Malheur National Forest, Oregonl received considerable damage over the winter months. The gate at the base of the lookout was torn off, and a nearby sign was completely destroyed. 'Structural supports for very important weather recording equipment also sustained damage.' it was added." *(Blue Mountain Eagle)*

⛰️

November 4, 1978: The lookout's cab [West White Pine, Roosevelt National Forest, Coloradol was removed to Lee Martinez City Park in Fort Collins by the Army Reserve using a helicopter.

⛰️

1978: "All windows and casings were destroyed and a hole burned in the cabin floor. Graffiti on the remaining walls gave mute testimony of disrespect [Snow Peak, Linn County Fire Patrol, Oregonl." *(Linn District Annual Report)*

⛰️

May 18, 1983: "The U.S. Forest Service reported a 300-gallon water tank was stolen from the Bald Mountain Lookout station [Eldorado National Forest, Californial off Wentworth Springs Road sometime during the winter. The theft was discovered May 15." *(Mountain Democrat)*

⛰️

May 21, 1986: "Rocks were thrown at a U.S. Forest Service weather station on Bald Mountain [Eldorado National Forest, Californial between May 17 and 18, causing an estimated $360 worth of damage, according to sheriff's reports." *(Mountain Democrat)*

⛰️

July 3, 1991: "U.S. Forest Service officials reported June 29 that the fire lookout tower at Thompson Peak [Plumas National Forest, Californial had been vandalized. No estimation of the damage was available." *(Feather River Bulletin)*

⛰️

May 24, 1992: "Vandals attempted to burn a caretaker cabin and damaged a fire tower atop Blue Mountain [Hamilton County, New York] earlier this month, Department of Environmental Conservation officials reported Friday.

DEC is investigating, but officials are unsure if the incident is related to the toppling of the Pharoah Mountain tower in mid-April.

DEC Ranger Greg George of Blue Mountain Lake said a hiker discovered May 10 that someone has broken into the observers cabin and dragged all of the furniture and bedding outside where it was burned. Vandals also smashed porch bannisters and tried to burn the cabin, but only succeeded in charring the interior. He said the lock was broken and windows were smashed in the booth atop the fire tower.

Tower legs were not cut as they were on the Pharaoh Mountain structure, nor were there any apparent attempts at structural damage, George reported." *(Press-Republican)*

Dry Soda

Malheur National

Forest, Oregon

August 2009

Ron Kemnow Photo

October 24, 1992: "A Thursday night fire that destroyed the Alabama Forestry Commission's Barton fire tower [Alabama] was intentionally set, state Fire Marshall Richard Montgomery confirmed Friday. Seven other grass fires ignited in the same vicinity at about the same time and ranged from 3 feet in diameter to an acre in size.

Montgomery said although no physical evidence was left behind that would link the fire to arson, "there was no doubt in my mind."

'I'm 99 percent sure that it was arson' Montgomery said. 'We found no accidental cause for it. We took burned debris samples and sent them to the Huntsville forensic science lab.'

Montgomery said the lab results will determine the cause of the fire and whether or not a liquid or other substance was used in arson.

He said insurance adjustors were on the scene Friday to assess damages but a final estimate was not released. However, he said in his estimation damages were probably between $10,000 and $12,000.

According to Montgomery, the fire tower— a small, concrete building at the top of Mount Mills Road or Barton Mountain— will have to be replaced, along with two radios used by state forestry officials.

Alabama Forestry Commission district forester Gerald Steeley said one grass fire was reported at about 7:30 p.m., and when Barton firefighters contacted a forestry official, he in turn tried to contact their tower to no avail.

'Our ranger discovered that the radio was out the tower and he went to check it out' Steeley said. 'When he got there he found the building gone.'

No one was injured in the fire.

Steeley said his department has had problems with vandalism at the tower in the past, but this is the first time a fire occurred there.

Colbert County Sheriff Buddy Ald _____ said two suspects were being questioned Friday in relation to the fire. He said his department is investigating the fire, which was determined to have started in the roof area and spread downward.

Montgomery said people that set fires on government property 'obviously don't realize that they're the very ones who will have to pay for it.'

'Any time state property is damaged, we're going to have to pay for it some way, in taxes or some other way,' he said. 'They're the ones that will have to pay for it." *(Times Daily)*

February 10, 1996: Arsonists burned the lookout [Hanging Rock, Monroe County, West Virginia] on the night of the 10th.

November 16, 1997: "The Quartz Mountain lookout, situated on a ridge at 4,830-feet, six miles southeast of Republic, burned to the ground on Oct. 7. Colville National Forest officials say the cabin and 30-foot tower fell victim to arson." *(The Spokesman-Review)*

August 9, 2002: "The U.S. Forest Service Bald Mountain Lookout [Eldorado National Forest, California] on Country Road was burglarized July 31. A generator, power converter and chain saw were taken. The estimated loss is $2,000." *(Mountain Democrat)*

August 27, 2002: "Northern Idaho's Black Mounain is closed because there is no money to repair recent vandalism." *(Bonner County Daily Bee)*

August 28, 2002: "Black Mountain Lookout in Boundary County [Idaho] was vandalized in early august and more than two dozen large trees around the lookout were cut down.

Someone used a chain saw to make cuts part way through a main crossbeam of the support structure and on sections of the hand rail on the tower,; stated Lynn Kaney, Acting District Ranger at the Bonners Ferry Ranger District.

It appears the vandalism took place sometime before Wednesday, Aug. 7. The first report of the damage came from visitors who had rented the lookout for an overnight stay." *(Bonner County Daily Bee)*

December 15, 2005: "Nine windows have been broken out of the Lorena Butte Lookout [Department of Natural Resources, Washington; Private] near Goldendale, according to a man who reported it to the Klickitat County Sheriff's Office.

Matt LeFever, 21, believes the damage may have been caused by kids who told him they are in sixth grade.

LeFever, who lives next to the lookout, told police that he drove two kids to the Goldendale Library at approximately 4:15 p.m. Monday from near the lookout. He said he gave them a ride because they appeared to be 'freezing' on the roadside.

He said he passed two other kids on the outskirts of town. He also said four sets of tracks were visible in the snow going to and from the lookout.

LeFever said he learned of the broken windows from the kids, who told him they were broken out of the structure.

Now on private property, the lookout was erected in 1953, said LeFever, who has been restoring it for several years." *(The Goldendale Sentinel)*

April 4, 2006: "Vandals destroyed the historic Mount Sexton fire lookout [Josephine County, Oregon] and three Oregon Department of Forestry repeater antennas Saturday night. (April 1st)

The damage, which included three structures and other communications equipment, could total as much as $500,00, according to an Oregon State Police detective leading the investigation." *(Medford Mail Tribune)*

🏔

2006: Over the 4th of July weekend vandals broke into the lookout and caused significant damage [High Ridge, Umatilla National Forest, Oregon].

🏔

2008: The lookout [Harriet's Peak, Department of Natural Resources, Washington] was discovered toppled over; upon inspection the action may have been helped by the loosening of leg clamps.

🏔

2010: Thieves stripped all the copper lightning protection wire from the tower. As a result the tower could not be staffed this season. [South Baldy Mountain, Colville National Forest, Washington]

High Ridge

Umatilla National Forest

Oregon

July 2008

Ron Kemnow Photo

April 15, 2011: The lookout was burned by the Maine Department of Conservation, citing vandalism and other distractions as a reason for the removal.

🏔

October 2012: During the first part of the month the lookout structure [Kloshe Nanich, Olympic National Forest, Washington] was removed.

Reason for the removal was the advance state of deterioration and recent vandalism. With budgets tight the only recourse was to remove a potential hazard to the public.

Spring 2012: The cause of a fire that destroyed the lookout structure [Bosley Butte, Curry County, Oregon] is still under investigation (mid-May). Vandalism is suspected.

2012: The vandalized remains of the lookout structure were removed [Grizzly Peak, Shasta-Trinity National Forest, California].

November 22, 2013: A report was published that thieves vandalized and broke into the tower [Mount Bemm, Gippsland, Victoria, Australia]. The thieves cut through a chain link fence, then cut through the manhole allowing them to climb the tower where they drilled out some rivets and kicked the door in. The report states that in addition to the vandalism two radios were stolen, thus compromising the lookouts ability to function with the fire season approaching. *(Source: www.timbull.com.au)*

Bosley Butte

Curry County

Oregon

July 24, 2008

Ron Kemnow

Photo

2013: The lookout was converted into an all steel viewing platform for public use. The incidence of vandalism of the original structure prompted the expenditure of approximately $23,000 to retain one of the last two lookouts in the county.

October 29, 2014: An account of vandalism was reported in the local news. A person climbed the 20-metre (approximately 65-foot) ladder to destroy the lock and badly damaged the access (trap) door. Also the security fence was damaged and a window received a bullet hole. The damage has been repaired and the lookout will be ready for the fire season. *[Collins, Department of Parks and wildlife, Western Australia]*

December 12, 2014: During a recent staff inspection, the fire tower [Mount Nugong, Gippsland DEPI, Victoria, Australia] was discovered to have been vandalized. The damage included wire fencing being cut, the ceiling hatch forced open, two solar panels broken and a winch was removed from its mounting and dropped to the concrete at the base of the tower. This vandalism adds an unnecessary maintenance expense prior to the fire season.

May 20, 2015: The tower and Towerman's cabin on Stratton Mountain [Green River National Forest, Vermont] were vandalized some time before May 16. The U.S. Forest Service asking for help in its investigation Both structures are listed on the National Register of Historic Places and are prominent landmarks along both the Appalachian Trail and Vermonts Long Trail.

2015: Between wind damage and vandalism, the lookout [Thompson Peak, Plumas National Forest, California] has been closed until repairs can be made. An alternate fire watch arrangement has been taken.

September 3, 2016: The lookout [Little Snowy Top, Kaniksu National Forest, Idaho] was burned to the ground during the afternoon hours. The fire is believed to be the result of carelessness of people using the building for shelter.

September 2016: Just prior to the Labor Day weekend the New Jersey Department of Environmental Protection erected a barrier to block access to the tower [Apple Pie Hill, Wharton State Forest]. Reason stated for this action was that vandalism, theft and unsavory activities have been increasing over the past several years. The total cost of the fence, approximately $200.00.

www.ingramcontent.com/pod-product-compliance
Lightning Source LLC
Chambersburg PA
CBHW060055050426
42448CB00011B/2465